THIS BOOK
BELONGS TO:

For all four-legged friends

Special thanks to:

Judy, Kit, Helena, Alex, Chris, David Witt,
Victoria and Rick Baker, Wild Spirit Wolf Sanctuary,
Nicole Schepker, Rory Zoerb, Robin Walters and Julie Seton.

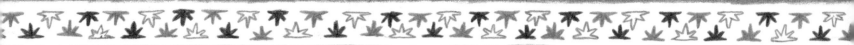

THE WOLVES
OF CURRUMPAW

WILLIAM GRILL

FLYING EYE BOOKS
LONDON ✦ NEW YORK

UNITED STATES
OF AMERICA

NEW MEXICO

CONTENTS

THE OLD WEST

New Mexico, 1862

Half a million wolves once roamed freely across North America, but with the arrival of European settlers the habitats of the animals began to change.

These were the dying days of the old west and the fate of wolves was sealed in it.

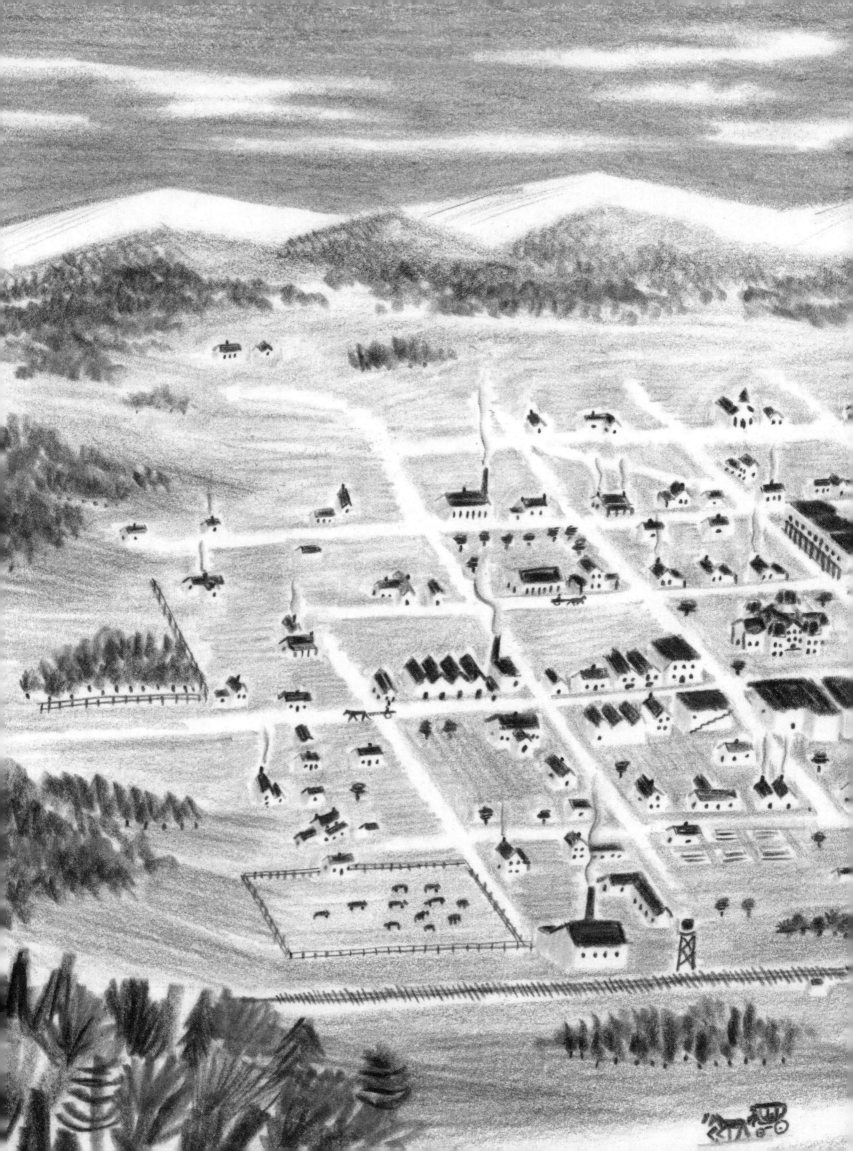

A few, however, still roamed the vast and changing landscape.

THE KING OF CURRUMPAW

Currumpaw, 1893

Old Lobo or the King, as the natives called him, was the great leader of a notorious pack of grey wolves. For over five years his reign of terror had been felt across the Currumpaw valley.

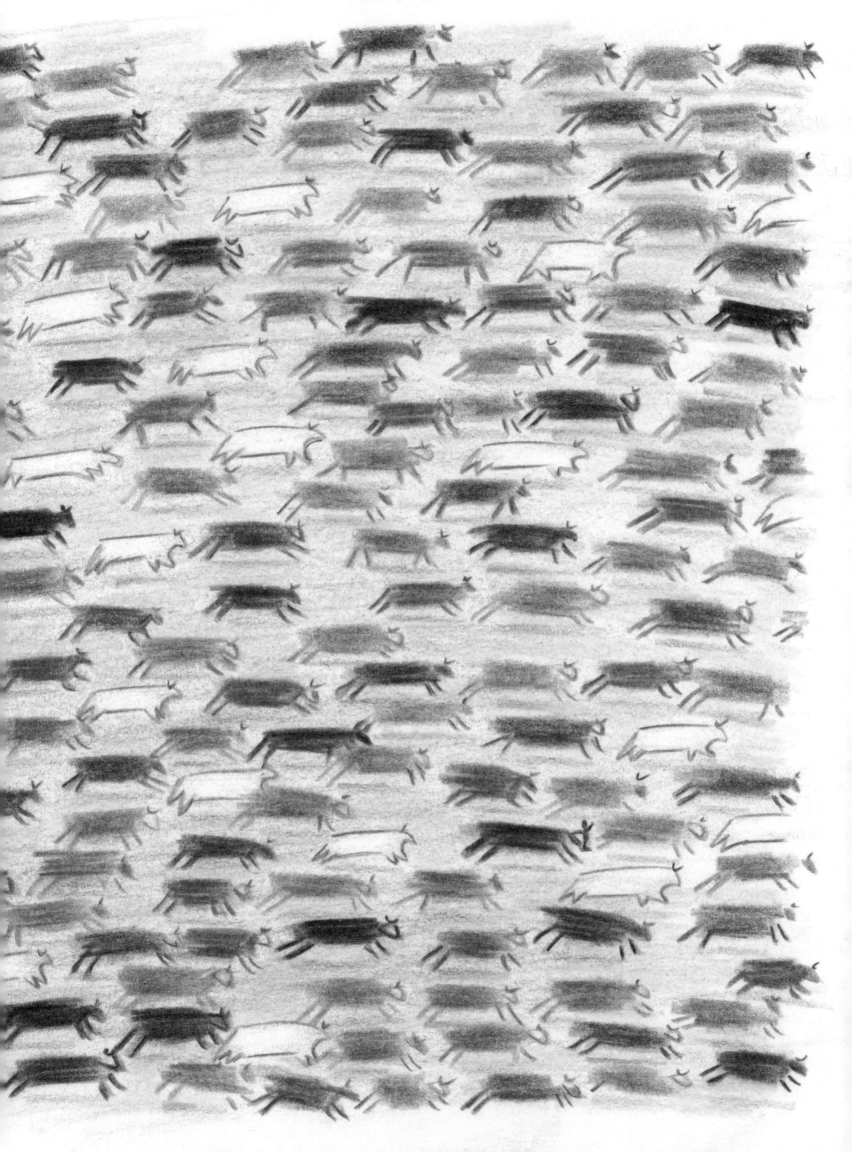

LOBO

GREY WOLF

BLANCA

THE PACK

Old Lobo was a giant among wolves who commanded a sleek and well-conditioned pack: each of them was a wolf of renown. Lobo's band was a small one, but fiercely loyal to their leader. At night his deep howl struck fear through the hearts of the ranchmen and farmers, as they knew it meant yet another raid on their cattle.

SETON

LALOCHE

TANNERY

CALONE

FARMERS

THE FITZ RANDOLPHS

RANCHMEN
AND STOCKMEN

Every cattle baron and cowboy in the land wanted Lobo dead. The ranchmen believed that he and his pack possessed charmed lives and couldn't be caught. And so, a bounty of $1000 was placed on Lobo's head: a sum unheard of at the time.

One day a Texas Ranger named Tannery came thundering into Currumpaw. Tannery and his large pack of wolf-hounds had killed many wolves out on the plains of Texas, and he was confident he'd soon have the old bandit's scalp. At first light the hunt was under way and soon the wolf-hounds picked up the scent of the wolves.

However, the country here was different to back home in Texas. Using the range to their advantage, Lobo and his pack split, scattering Tannery and his 29 dogs among the rocky canyons and tributaries.

At nightfall only six hounds returned to Tannery, two of which were badly wounded. After a further two failed attempts to capture the outlaws, Tannery eventually fled back to Texas, disgraced and embarrassed.

The following year, two more hunters tried their hand at capturing the royal hide, each of them certain the bounty would soon be theirs. Laloche, a French Canadian, believed Lobo was not simply a wolf but a genuine "loup-garou" (werewolf), and therefore could not be caught by ordinary means. He cleverly created his own devious poisons, and used a whole array of spells, charms and incantations, each more elaborate than the last. Day in, day out, he tried and tried, but for all his tricks Lobo eluded him.

Joe Calone, a local farmer, had devised a new poison. It had already claimed 100 wolves in half a year. But Old Lobo scorned his enemies. For each trap and poison bait laid, he returned the favour by ravaging Calone's cattle. This humiliation alone was not enough for Lobo. Within a thousand yards of Calone's house, Lobo made his den and raised his family, taking Calone's cattle as he pleased. Exasperated and ashamed, Calone retreated...

...leaving old Lobo as ever the ruler of the plains.

THE WOLF HUNTER

New York City, 1893

Thousands of miles away, a revered wolf-hunter and British naturalist by the name of Ernest Thompson Seton spent his days hunched over his desk, yearning to be under open skies.

His family had emigrated from England to Canada when he was a young boy. Amongst the solace of the trees he had spent many hours observing and drawing animals. Over time he became increasingly interested in hunting animals, as it allowed him to make authentic observational drawings. The older he grew, the thicker his skin became.

By the age of 33 he had become an accomplished artist and a reputable hunter. He was an expert when it came to wolves, having grown up with them on the Canadian frontier and then hunting them for bounty money countless times. He had even written a concise guide to catching them and proclaimed with pride that one of his Scottish ancestors had wiped out the last remaining wolves in Britain.

The city had begun to take its toll and hours of concentrated drawing was becoming unhealthy. Seton's doctor advised him to take a break from work.

Upon hearing from a land owner called Fitz Randolph about the problems on his ranch in Clayton, New Mexico, Seton leapt at the chance to leave the city.

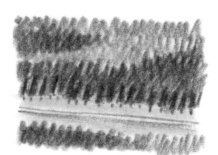

When Seton arrived in Clayton, Fitz Randolph had a horse and lodging ready and was waiting for 130 wolf traps to arrive. Seton was intent on waging a campaign of traps and poison against Lobo. He was well equipped for the task with items such as a box camera, clothing covered in dried blood, a bone knife, and his journal.

Determined to succeed where the others had failed, Seton spent some time getting to know Lobo's territory first. Every day he made new friends and discovered new animals across the prairie.

In time he came to understand these wolves were most scrupulous about what they ate. The ranchmen told him they shunned any animal that had died from natural causes, especially anything killed by a stockman. The wolves had learned that evidence of a human hand meant deception.

They disliked mutton, horseflesh, old bulls or cows, and even young colts. Their choice was always a freshly killed heifer.

Tannery had proved the country was too rough to use horses and dogs. So Seton set out using poison until large enough traps arrived. He took every precaution in preparing the baits, using the technique of a master trapper. He disguised strychnine and cyanide poisons in a mixture of cheese and fat, which was inserted into a piece of meat.

He rode out across the mesa making a ten-mile circuit, dropping bait every quarter of a mile. As darkness fell he heard King Lobo's deep howl. One of the cowboys sat up, "There he is, we'll see."

When morning came they soon picked up the trail of the cunning thieves. Seton could tell Lobo's track immediately. It measured 5 1/2 inches claw to heel, an inch longer than any ordinary wolf. From this he was able to calculate he weighed around 78 lbs.

With keen eyes he scanned the tracks. The first bait was gone, as was the second and the third! The cunning devil... Seton couldn't believe his eyes. Old Lobo had stacked all three baits on top of the fourth and scattered filth over them in disrespect. Again and again Seton tried to deceive him, but the old king wolf was too wise.

After many more failed attempts, poison was proving useless. The only thing it achieved was suffering to other creatures. One day, Seton could only watch helplessly as the cruel poison took hold of a coyote.

He put out no more baits.

Without any sight of his foe, Seton asked the foreman where he might go hunting. "Ain't much to hunt round here but snipes," the man said, "everything's been killed off." Once the plains had swelled with bison, antelope and deer. Now there was but a small bison herd a few miles away; were these the last survivors of the frontier?

Seton realised that the starved wolves were praying upon the cattle because they didn't have a choice. But Lobo's mocking howl still haunted Seton, and knowing that his reputation as a master trapper was at stake, he persisted.

BLANCA

January 25th, 1894

Finally the traps arrived and with the help of a
cowboy, Seton set to work. For one long week they
set out every device at their disposal.

The next day Seton rode out to inspect. There in the dust he could read the story of the previous night. In the darkness Lobo had tip-toed amongst the traps and invisible as they were, he had somehow detected them. He had carefully scratched and kicked up the earth until the trap was disarmed, and continued until he had disabled every other trap laid on the trail.

The same situation played out no matter how many times the traps were reconfigured and disguised. Seton began to wonder if the old wolf could ever be deceived; Lobo's intellect and cunning was unlike any wolf he had previously encountered.

Weeks passed... Almost at
the point of giving up, Seton
noticed something unusual
about the Currumpaw pack...

... there were smaller tracks
in the dust, ahead of Lobo's.
How could this be?

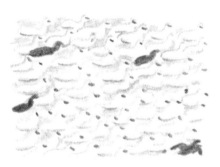

"I saw them today," a cowboy remarked, "the one who breaks away is Blanca."

Of course! Blanca must be a she-wolf... The old bandit was in love,
Seton thought. A male wolf would never leave his mate's side.

A treacherous new plan emerged.

With a cowboy's assistance, Seton rigged two obvious
traps around the carcass of a freshly killed heifer.

Then he placed the head apart, accompanied by two of his best, most well disguised traps.
Afterwards he combed the dust with a coyote hide and made tracks with one of the paws.

The trap was ready. But this time it wasn't Lobo that Seton was hoping to trap...

In the crisp morning light, they rode out with eager eyes. As expected,
Lobo had kept his pack from harm. But the tracks of a smaller wolf had
deviated from the pack, and moments later they found her.

At first sight she bolted, making ground despite the trap.
Encumbered by the fifty-pound heifer head, she was soon held fast by rocks.

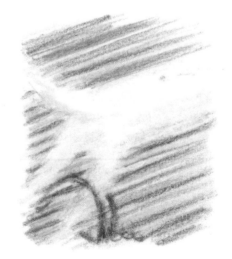

Blanca was the most beautiful wolf Seton had ever seen. She turned to face
him and let out a rallying cry, her howl reverberating across the canyon.
From over the mesa replied the deep call of Lobo, but he was too far away.

She made her last cry as they closed in.
With a heavy heart, Seton loaded her carefully onto his horse.

Lobo's howl echoed throughout the distant land as he desperately searched for Blanca. He hadn't really deserted her, but seeing the men's guns he knew he could not save her.

All day long Seton and the ranchmen heard him calling. "Now, indeed, I truly know that Blanca is his mate," remarked Seton.

Finding the spot where Blanca had taken her last breath, his wailing rolled far over the canyon. Even the ever stoic cowboys turned their heads.

Old Lobo seemed to know exactly what had happened and taking up the men's trail he followed it up to the ranch-house. In cold-blooded revenge he set upon the ranch's watchdog and left him in small pieces.

The next morning Seton found Old Lobo's reckless trail. He had been caught in one of the traps, but had somehow managed to free himself. If Seton was ever going to catch the wolf, he would have to strike now while Lobo was off balance.

Using all 130 wolf traps, Seton set to work straightaway. The scent of Blanca would be used to lure Lobo closer to the ranch. The men worked tirelessly until there was nothing left to do, and as the sun fell Seton waited.

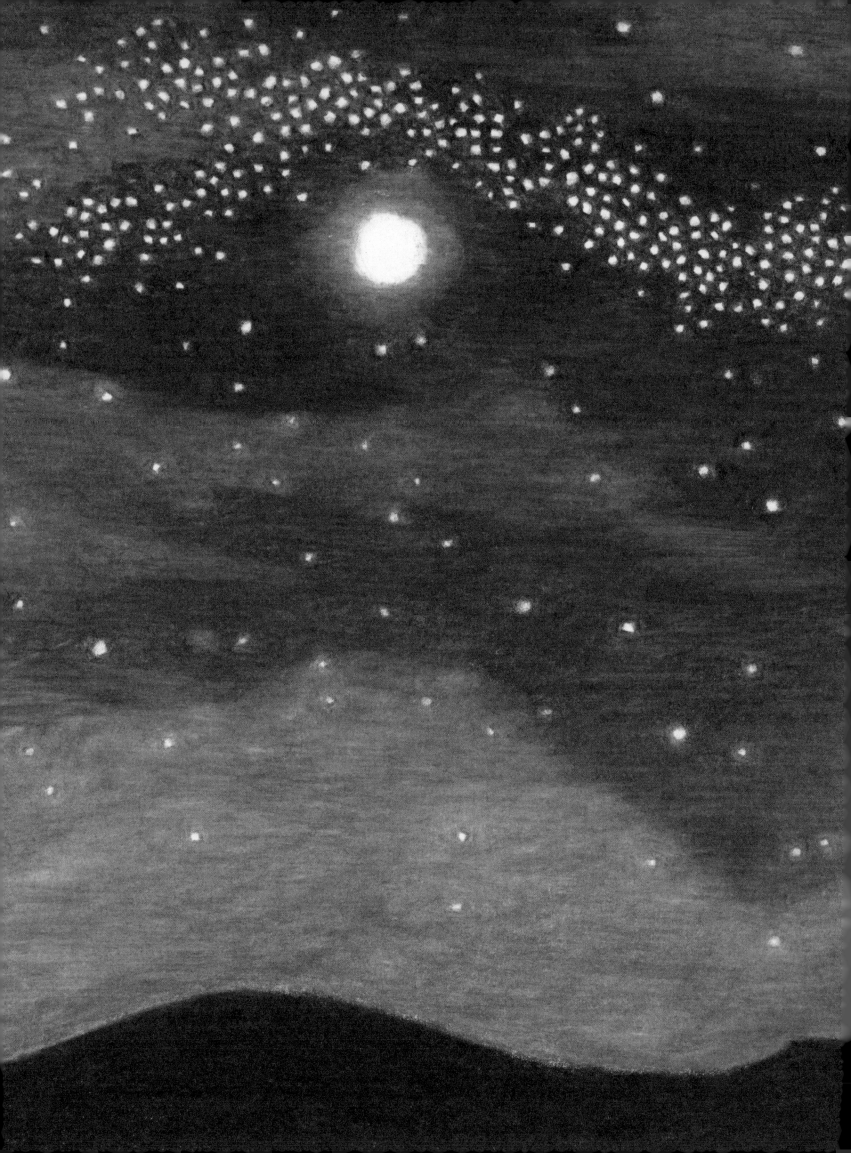

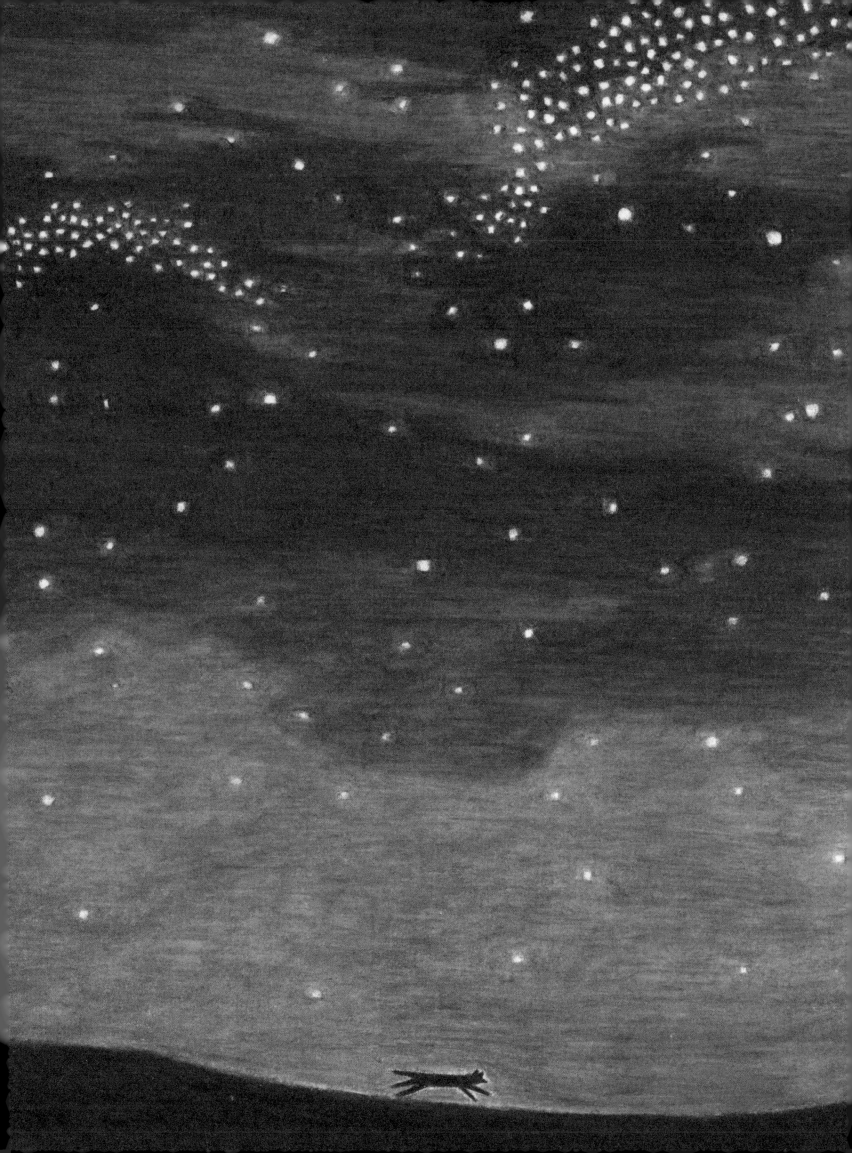

The following day Seton searched the canyons and the mesas but found nothing.

"There was a great row among the cattle this morning," one of the cowboys said during supper. "Maybe there is something in the traps there."

The next afternoon Seton rode out. Upon reaching
the brow of the hill the great outlaw came into view.

CAPTURE

January 31st, 1894

Lobo, the King of Currumpaw, stood defiantly in
the traps. As Seton approached, he rose up and let out
a deep roar. Yet there was no one to answer him.

"Grand old outlaw, hero of a thousand lawless raids,
in a few minutes you will be but a great load of carrion.
It cannot be otherwise," Seton murmured.

Yet before the light had died in Lobo's fierce eyes, Seton suddenly cried,
"Stay, we will not kill him; let us take him alive to the camp."

Lobo's breath came evenly as though sleeping, but his eyes were bright and clear again. They were fixed on the great rolling mesas, towards his passing kingdom where his famous band were now scattered.

Back at the ranch-house, Lobo's bindings were removed and the men fitted him with a collar and chain. For the first time Seton was able to examine him and dispel the rumours that demonised him. There were no supernatural markings, no collar of gold around his neck – he was just a grand old wolf with battle scars.

Old Lobo refused water and food. He lay still, breathing slowly
with his eyes resting on the far away plains, his plains. As the
sun went down, no call went out to his band. He remained silent
and still.

"A lion shorn of his strength, an eagle robbed of his freedom, or a dove bereft of his mate, all die, it is said, of a broken heart; and who will avert that this grim bandit could bear the three-fold brunt, heart-whole?" wrote Seton later.

As the sun rose the following morning Lobo remained quiet and still, but the great strength and spirit in him had gone – the old King wolf was dead.

Seton had achieved what he set out to do, but now understanding the true nature of the wolf he was stricken with shame. The chain was removed from Lobo's neck and he was carried to the shed where Blanca lay.

As they laid him beside her, the cowboy murmured sorrowfully, "There, you would come to her, now you are together again."

A CHANGED MAN

February 4th, 1894

This story doesn't end with King Lobo's death. Although gone, his legacy lives on. Seton was a deeply conflicted man, torn between his love of nature and his cunning ability as a hunter. However, after the death of Lobo, something in him changed.

"This proved to be one of the turning points of my life..." he reflected, and immediately wrote *Lobo: The King of Currumpaw,* where he cast himself as the villain and Lobo as the hero. Seton devoted the rest of his life to protecting the wolf species, and to the conservation of American wildlife that was so heavily under threat.

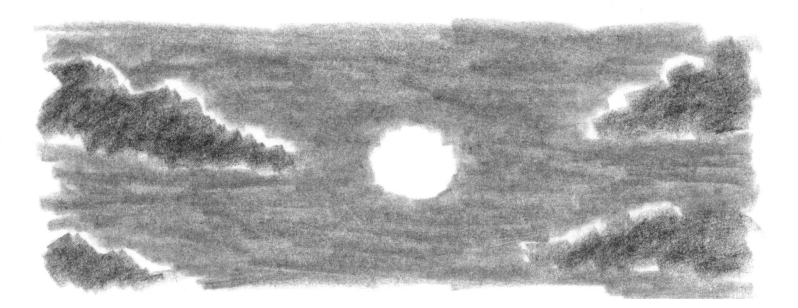

He never killed a wolf again.

In 1902 Seton founded the Woodcraft Indians. He believed that "through the promotion of interest in outdoor life and woodcraft lies the preservation of wildlife and landscape".

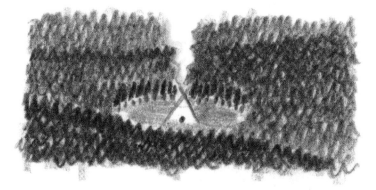

After the success of the Woodcraft movement, Seton broadened his reach and became a founding member of the boy scouts of America. He never rested, and his work led the way for many to follow.

Sadly, humans continued to hunt wolves and their species almost vanished, but Seton had started a fire that would spread throughout the American consciousness.

Inspired by his work, biologists, writers, and ecologists gradually followed Seton's trail, each contributing to the cause of wolves in their own way. Seton had become a key part of a new frontier: the conservation movement.

ADOLF MURIE

ALDO LEOPOLD

FARLEY MOWAT

DOUGLAS W. SMITH

DAVID ATTENBOROUGH

L. DAVID MECH

They argued that the removal of wolves was not only unethical but also damaging to the environment. Slowly, people began to see wolves as intelligent, loyal creatures capable of meaningful relationships, while also serving a positive purpose in the ecosystem.

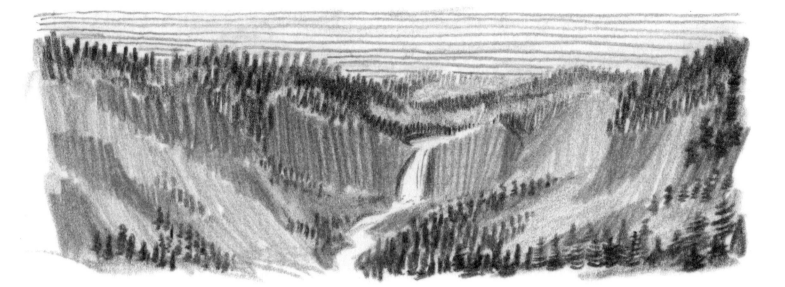

In 1973 the grey wolf became protected under the endangered species act. Wolf sanctuaries were slowly emerging and in 1995, fourteen wolves were reintroduced to Yellowstone National Park.

At an estimated population of 9,000 in the USA today, their journey hasn't been an easy one. But little by little, wolves have made progress by the will of a few remarkable people, including a hunter who decided to change his ways...

...and a 78 lb grey wolf called
Lobo, the King of Currumpaw.

"Ever since Lobo, my sincerest wish has been to impress upon people that each of our native wild creatures is in itself a precious heritage that we have no right to destroy or put beyond the reach of our children."

— Ernest Thompson Seton

GLOSSARY

Antelope

A deer-like animal with upward pointing horns.

Colt

A young male horse.

Bison

A large, wild animal of the cow family with curved horns and a humped back.

Coyote

An animal closely related to the grey wolf, but smaller. Their current population level is probably at the highest it's ever been.

Bull

An adult male cow.

Deer

A hooved mammal, with antlers growing on the males.

Calf
A young cow or bull.

Ecosystem

A complicated set of interactions between animals and plants in a particular environment.

Canyon

A deep valley between hills or mountains, usually with a stream running through it.

Endangered
When a species of animal is at risk of going extinct (disappearing completely).

Carrion

The dead or decaying flesh of an animal.

Grey Wolf

The largest of the wolf family, native to the wilderness and remote areas of North America.

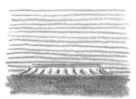

Heifer
A young cow, before she
has had her first calf.

Prairie
A large area of
open grassland.

Loup-Garou
The French word for werewolf;
a mythical human that can
transform into a wolf-like creature.

Settlers
The European explorers who
arrived and took over North
America in the 16th century.

Mesa
A hill with a flat top
and steep sides.

Snipe
A small wading bird with
short legs and a long bill.

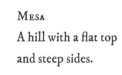

Natives
The indigenous American
Indian tribes who first lived
in New Mexico.

Trap
A device to catch animals.

Pasture
Land covered in grasses,
where animals graze.

Tributary
A stream or river that flows
into a larger river or lake.

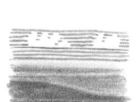

Plain
A large area of flat
and open land.

Wolf-hound
A large dog, often a
greyhound mix, used for
hunting wolves.

APPENDIX

AUTHOR'S NOTE

This story is based on Ernest Thompson Seton's original short story
Lobo: The King of Currumpaw, from his book *Wild Animals I Have Known*,
along with my own additional research into Seton and this period.
During Seton's time (1800s – early 1900s) people did not fully understand
the effect poison had on animals. Although wild animals are sometimes
hunted today, more humane methods are used.

BOOKS

Ernest Thompson Seton,
Wild Animals I Have Known, 1898

David L. Witt, *Ernest Thompson Seton: The Life
and Legacy of an Artist and Conservationist*, 2010

Ernest Thompson Seton, transcribed by Julie Seton,
*The Wolf Hunt, Seton's Personal Journal,
1893 – 1894*, 1995

Farley Mowat, *Never Cry Wolf*, 1963

Garry Marvin, *Wolf*, 2012

ONLINE

Defenders of Wildlife: *www.defenders.org*

International Wolf Centre: *www.wolf.org*

Wolf Worlds: *www.wolfworlds.com*

U.S. Fish & Wildlife Service: *www.fws.gov*

PLACES

WILD SPIRIT WOLF SANCTUARY, 378 Candy Kitchen Rd, Ramah, NM 87321, United States
PHILMONT MUSEUM & SETON MEMORIAL LIBRARY, 17 Deer Run Rd, Cimarron, NM 87714, United States
SETON CASTLE & THE ACADEMY FOR THE LOVE OF LEARNING, 133 Seton Village Rd, Santa Fe, NM 87508, United States
HERZSTEIN MEMORIAL MUSEUM, 22 S 2nd St, Clayton, NM 88415, United States
MUSEUM OF INDIAN ARTS AND CULTURE, 708 Camino Lejo, Santa Fe, NM 87505, United States

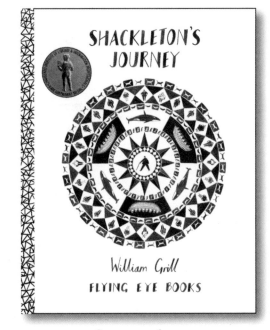

SHACKLETON'S JOURNEY

William Grill

FLYING EYE BOOKS

978-1-909263-10-9

"William Grill eschews panels for wonderfully immersive spreads. A book that captures the rewards and trials of polar exploration in great style."

— the Guardian

Published in the US by Nobrow (US) Inc.
Printed in Latvia on FSC assured paper.

ISBN: 978-1-909263-83-3
Order from www.flyingeyebooks.com